An Atlas of Commonplaces

Pablo Helguera

An Atlas of Commonplaces

A notebook for artists

Edited by Thyrza Nichols Goodeve

Jorge Pinto Books, Inc.
New York

An Atlas of Commonplace
A notebook for artists

© Pablo Helguera, 2015

All rights reserved. This book may not be reproduced in whole or in part, in any form (beyond copying permitted by Sections 107 and 108 of the United States Copyright Law, and except limited excerpts by reviewer for the public press), without written permission from Jorge Pinto Books Inc. 6216 Vorlich Lane, Bethesda, Maryland, 20816

© Copyright of the edition Jorge Pinto Books Inc. 2015.

Edited by Thyrza Nichols Goodeve

Cover image: © Pablo Helguera

Book typesetting: Charles King, website: www.ckmm.com

ISBN: 978-1-934978-84-9
ISBN-10: 1-934978-84-1

Foreword

This is a notebook that primarily reflects on the art practice, mostly with artists in mind. However, it is my hope that the aphorisms presented here may be of interest to a wider audience, as they try to provide a general sense of the issues on creativity, criticism, and value that are common in art today.

This book is also a result of the desire to comment on the increasing atomization of communication created by the rise of social media. The tweet, the meme, and the status report often replace the longer and more nuanced reflection on a given topic, which in turn require a slower pace of reflection and discussion. The question on whether it is possible to generate thoughtful commentary in a succinct manner, without trivializing or caricaturizing a topic of discussion, attracted me to the subject of the aphorism—the literary tradition of the pithy statement that contains much to be discussed even if it is presented in only a few words. As a test of how such a conversation could be triggered, I posted a few of the aphorisms in this book onto my Facebook page. Most of the phrases were met with a forceful debate and comments that ranged from supportive and enthusiastic to angry and critical, dominated by the lethal opinions of the relativists, such as "one can't generalize." In general, the readers seemed to overlook the whole point of the aphorist's tradition, which is that an aphorism is, in essence, a deliberate, but also strategic, game of generalization that can be easily questioned or objected to by someone unable to see the larger picture of a problem. In past years I have become involved in producing cartoons about the art world in the style of the New Yorker magazine, known as "single-panels," most of which contain a caption that often can be equated with the critical, or rather, opinionated, judgment contained in an aphorism. Because these drawings are understood as humor, it is generally accepted that they intend to exaggerate a particular situation or problem in order to effect their stinging criticism on an issue. However, when a single phrase, presented in a seemingly authoritative tone, is put out in public, there is often a much greater discomfort in accepting it, as the kind of reactions that I received on Facebook proved.

In some cases the statements did not necessarily represent a personal position, but rather a description of a collective attitude toward a problem. In this sense, *An Atlas of Commonplaces* is indebted to a literary tradition that includes Flaubert's *Dictionary of Received Ideas* and Swift's *Thoughts on Various Subjects*—both critical statements of intellectual attitudes of their times, but at the same time efforts of creating a taxonomy of bourgeois thought on a variety of topics.

It is inevitable, for any contemporary visual artist, to undertake a project like this without acknowledging Jenny Holzer's *Truisms*—a major body of work initiated in 1977 and which has taken many forms over the decades. Since that time, many of us adopted and assimilated many of Holzer's phrases such as "abuse of power comes as no surprise" and "protect me from what I want" into everyday conversation. I am indebted to Holzer in the way in which she took the format of the maxim and introduced it into conceptual art to produce a critique of power dynamics in today's society. So without pretending to present any kind of innovative form, this book is instead presented as a conscious continuation of an artistic tradition that is only different from the place and time in which it has ben produced, and in particular focusing on art as we live it today.

Brooklyn, November 2015

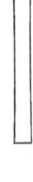

We should consider the fact the majority of great artists are great in spite of how dull their lives were.

When we make something of relevance, our contribution fares better if we label ourselves anonymous.

In his lifetime, he had one minor idea, but he took care of it with great tenderness and dedication. It turned into a beautiful career.

We spend too much time recognizing people and too little time understanding what they do.

Failure is overrated.

Please don't reward me for my successes, but admire me for my courage when I have failed.

The Exhibition of Misplaced Hopes: an exhibition of works by artists who were major figures in their lifetime but are utterly forgotten today.

Most of us survive failure; barely anyone survives success.

He made so many rules to live by he was immobilized.

Good artists perform miracles everyone can see. Great artists perform miracles most can't see.

Nobody is "ahead of their time". Visionaries simply change their present, while others passively inhabit it.

To counteract the possibility that he would never be recognized, he made his best effort to appear desirable, yet out of reach.

We look at the aspirational story of an artist who, at 89, is finally given her first solo museum, and at 100 is claimed to be a legend, as proof that perseverance wins out in the end. Yet how many artists remain utterly unknown in their lifetime?

The key to success is to stop being adventurous.

To become a hermit and retreat from the art world is rarely done as a strategy of resistance, but as a gesture of capitulation.

Making peace with the likelihood that I will be forgotten is a form of not believing in God.

The atheist should be more comfortable with failure.

Prominence is the one party to which no one is invited. You are only accepted if you sneak in.

We need to stop developing philosophies for success, and develop philosophies for failure.

When so many players are playing so many games, winning loses its meaning.

He decided he would remain an underdog, waiting for the right opportunity to achieve prominence, but the opportunity never came.

Some of the best ideas are born out of our belief that we have failed.

In the Land of the Forgettable Artists, the median artist stands out because those around him were less memorable.

Success is often the result of the alchemical mixture of the purest form of altruism with the darkest form of misanthropy.

We know full well that the notion of continued success is a fantasy, not so much because one could not theoretically produce great work all the time, but because we can't accept a narrative of permanent winners and permanent losers.

Rossini was famous for being lazy, and yet, he could compose a masterpiece in a matter of hours. This is not an excuse to be lazy, rather, it is a reminder to be as talented as Rossini.

In the end she realized she had lived the life of an imaginary artist who was known only to herself.

The concept of reinvention is mainly for those who weren't original in the first place.

He was one of the afflicted who tried to make a masterpiece with a single grand gesture.

Unsuccessful artists have nothing to hide, which is why they are unsuccessful.

He knew that his life would be unremarkable and boring, so he decided to promote his acceptance of this fact as a radical gesture. Subsequently he gained a great deal of attention, which ruined the radical impact of the original gesture.

Smart artists who succeed soon lose their smarts.

To be unnoticed does not make one undiscovered.

The easiest thing in the world is to break a rule in art; what is difficult is to become the rule in art.

If you find yourself justifying the reasons for making an artwork, you have already lost the argument.

Not evolving as an artist is just as bad as over-evolving.

The moment you get a handle on the subjects and approaches that define who you are as an artist, they tell you: "You are repeating yourself".

I have seen artists make great use of accidents. I have seen great artists whose entire career was an accident.

His success depended exclusively on how much he was able to be dissatisfied with the world.

The moment she forgot she was an artist she produced her best work.

He imagined a perfect artist who illustrated his ideas as if they were in a book, and then spent the rest of his life trying to become that artist.

His fame depended on testing recycled ideas that in the end were just bad ideas.

She was quick to identify artists whose work was trite, because she recognized herself in them.

His lack of talent would have remained a secret if he had not been so annoying.

Poor artists never forget.

We are the sum of our disappointments.

If only he had been forgotten, he would have been a great artist.

We should become connoisseurs of indifference.

The artists we despise most get all our attention.

The desire to remain relevant is both the most irrational and most natural impulse of an artist.

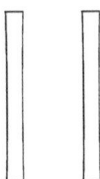

When we run out of ideas, we turn to celebrities.

The more we despise society, the more we seek its acceptance.

I am afraid to commit any crimes that may make me famous.

The farther we are from the stereotype, the more we inhabit it.

We don't need to look the part to be the part, we need to rewrite the part.

I have to perform several kinds of personas that are often afraid to bring them together. They come together when my fatigue overwhelms my fears.

People, not circumstances, are the greatest obstacle the artist must overcome.

It is not what matters to a group of people, but how they obscure what truly does.

By the time we die, we have been so many artists, our various identities could populate the art world.

The celebrity industry is an effective means of distribution, yet it is worthless when we have nothing to distribute.

It is demoralizing to see the manipulators, the fabricators of stories, and the celebrity-obsessed making headlines. As they define the zeitgeist and are the protagonists of our time, they also determine how we are understood.

Inner beauty is the fantasy realm we invoke when we have nothing positive to say about the world around us.

Both the artist and the criminal disregard the world and yet are desperate for acceptance.

We are the provincial inhabitants of of a little village known as the art world.

We spend so much time constructing our own mythical personas we end up no longer knowing who we are.

As artists, we dream of being in the limelight, only to realize it is just another form of invisibility.

The true test of an artist is what he or she does after achieving renown.

As artists we are at our best when we work like architects, not when we pose as theorists or craftsmen.

The goal is not to make objects people like, but to make objects people call their own.

We are giants of our own biographies.

The point of making art is to produce ideas that transform the ideas and material reality of others.

Not understanding an artwork doesn't prevent us from admiring it.

Relativism is best for making ignorant conclusions.

Fame is the most sought-after punishment.

An artist's life is one of internal debates, bureaucracy and routine.

Making viewers feel they are in control is the best approach.

The best way to determine how artists want to be perceived is by listening to their complaints.

Developing a sense of belonging is important, but it is even more important to develop a sense of not belonging.

Did everyone think we were just faking?

Inducing boredom is a necessary strategy.

An artist is a savage creature raised and protected by civilized ones.

Art is a terrible mirror of reality, yet it is a great manifestation of the theater of reality.

When we justify our right to make an artwork, we are merely trying to justify its relevance.

There are those who enter society burdened by the need to tell the world they are not as they appear. They fare better than those who are so confident, they never feel obligated to explain who they are.

Circumstances define us (Ortega). But we are the authors, and scapegoats, of those circumstances.

He attended social events in order to remind others how everyone was beneath him.

There is something suspicious about successful artists who look physically great, as if the process of making work had no verifiable impact in them.

Allow your first impressions to deceive you.

When you make art to prove that everything is a charade, it has no effect, because the charade is more accurate than any attempt to unmask it.

The greatest gift we can give to ourselves is to be as demanding as possible.

The most ambitious artists are also the best at projecting false modesty.

At a dinner party, everyone is an undiscovered author.

Our greatest sin is the way we despise the very public whose adoration we seek.

I am tired of this repressive society that allows me to do whatever I want.

To critique from the outside is like being radical while living in a comfortable suburb.

It is essential to feign madness and eccentricity as proof of our dedication.

There is a relationship between a society's tastes and its attention span.

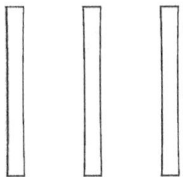

The wisdom of the Tao: "the way to be is to do", which is why artists live vicariously through the labor of their assistants.

Productivity is no antidote for the panic of feeling inconsequential.

We should never allow ourselves to sit and wait until an event that offends us is over.

Inhabiting the commonplace means we have found our Arcadia.

Is there such a thing as a virtuoso in conceptual art?

By calling it "art" it is now at a disadvantage.

Too much motivation is detrimental to the health of an artwork.

For all our desire for totality, we are required to work in fragments.

We are nostalgic for when it meant something to be committed to an idea.

For all the time we spend training artists, we should spend even more time training the public.

He spent his career beating a dead horse.

We must break every convention, including the convention that we must break every convention.

It is an obligation to be an artist so one can escape one's obligations.

Discontent is most unfortunate when it is inspired by the competition to outwit the superiority of another's idea.

Being an artist is not a professional choice —it is not a choice, period.

His ideas were microscopic; his sculpture monumental.

To be editors of our work we must imagine it is not our work.

Many people could make art from their daily lives if they were not so busy living those lives.

He took his mission in life too seriously and his daily work not seriously enough.

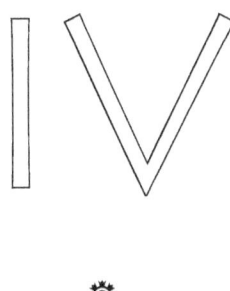

If you regard art education as a product that will transform you into a good artist, you are not an art producer but an art consumer.

When will we produce a system of knowledge instead of a system of passwords?

If we are incapable of gaining a following as an artist, we create one as a teacher.

Teaching is the activity with the greatest potential to produce independent and strong thinkers, but it is also where doctrine and dogma are born.

Rancière's *The Ignorant Schoolmaster* has by now become an elegant excuse for arguing that students can learn on their own.

An uncle of mine once said that teaching is only for bad artists, because good artists don't need teachers, just suggestions.

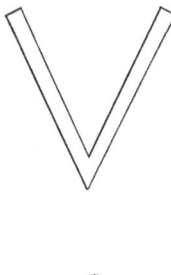

Monetary profit in art justifies itself in mysterious ways.

Wealthy art patrons may have good intentions, but they tend to mistake a world of fantasy and imagination for something tangible.

Subjective value is so amorphous that we seek to give it meaning with money.

It is tiresome to encounter an artist who expects acclaim because of his privilege.

We punish those who practice moderation in art-making because it reminds us that we are terrified of excess.

When an artwork is controversial we know it has value.

In the pristine realm of art, it is the dirtiest material that can have the best shine.

By the time his work was in fashion, he had already considered it unfashionable.

The artist is not a privileged individual, but someone born with a chronic condition.

If we could separate ourselves from our biases, we would stop being interested in art.

Never mistake hard-headedness for conviction.

VI

Artists are effective at being observers of the world but ineffective at being observers of themselves.

Those who believe they have all the answers should refrain from trying to become an artist.

Skepticism is the main ingredient one needs to achieve absolute paralysis.

"This is not about sound bytes", says the artist who can't stop talking.

Pretending that we know the meaning of something when we don't, is way more effective than knowing something and hiding it.

If everyone is right, but I can't join them, then at least I should learn to value the loneliness of my opinions.

We misplace objects in the same way we misplace opinions about art.

Make your texts impossible to understand so that we may suspect you are brilliant.

When her family protested that she used their horror stories as the subject of her art, she complained they were not supportive of her as an artist.

It is painful not to be recognized for the ingenuity of our manipulations.

One receives the important gifts from those who we take for granted.

She used inspirational and enlightening phrases all the time, which drew attention to the way inspiration and enlightenment always eluded her.

It is tempting to reject the art world with its contradictions and defects. But those who refuse to engage in the daily dynamics of art often become similar to the inhabitants of a black and white world, theorizing and gathering all the available information about a remote world in color, but without having ever experienced it in person.

We are always searching for one line best able to explain a work of art. Wouldn't it be better to use that one line to add complexity to the work?

When events like Katrina or Ayotzinapa occur, we realize how insignificant we actually are.

When we try to be polite by saying "it's not for me", we are really saying our taste is better.

Most of us are completely asleep; those who claim they are awake are merely speaking in their sleep.

Stupidity is addictive.

Part of being a visionary is being unaware that one is a visionary.

Elegant restraint is the disguise of the coward.

The first thing we should teach those who know nothing about art is that there is nothing crucial to know — and then let them spend the rest of their lives studying works of art.

Pay attention to the things that no one else sees.

The next revolution will be art that firmly takes control of our thoughts and emotions, instructing us exactly what to think and feel.

At some point, the most important ideas must feel the most banal.

To identify a problem while in the moment requires supreme insight; but to see it from the distance of time is something that even a child can do.

Those who have something to say are often crippled by doubt; they speak with hesitation, while those who have nothing to say bellow their ideas without hesitation.

The way we interpret someone's silence is just as important as the way we interpret that person's statements.

They attack a well-known artist saying his work is not art, not realizing that saying so does him a favor.

He consistently made so many wrong choices that he found it more viable to claim he had made them intentionally.

They thought his jokes were wonderful because it never occurred to them they were their very inspiration.

Those who know nothing about art are the first to argue that all art is subjective.

A visual artist is someone who doesn't listen.

He had all the references, all the artist names, all the anecdotes, and knew all the exhibitions but he had no clue what to do with this information.

We are quick to represent things that we don't understand.

"I don't work hard, I work smart", said he. But he wasn't smart enough to realize he needed to work harder at working to be smart.

Aim to be carefully careless.

The easy thing is to present things as they are, what's difficult is to present ourselves as we are.

The process of making great art is excruciatingly difficult, but once it is achieved the process appears to be simple.

We work hard not to make the same mistakes of those who came before us, only to make different mistakes and spend our lives pretending we have made none.

Just because no one could understand him, he thought he was a genius.

The timing of art is not causal, nor logical, nor does it necessarily coincide with the moment.

Artists who act as rebels will be considered idiots until they prove the intellectual and artistic basis of their rebellion.

There should be no pride in being an artist.

VII

Today we pay to have our ego stroked. These services are called degrees, gallery exhibitions, and paid subscriptions to *Who's Who*.

We relish our solitary battle in art only as long as the whole world knows about it.

Spectacle is the message.

I once was told by a famous artist: "You must give yourself to art 100%". She had given herself to narcissism 100%.

Save us from the tyranny of the righteous.

What if we only exhibited the artists' intentions, instead of the artists' works?

Make the other's pains yours, then take credit for your empathy.

Artists want to be present at their own funeral.

It is unfortunate that we can't make art without ourselves.

Solipsism is the most fashionable form of professional suicide.

"Show your wounds and they may be healed", someone once wrote, unconcerned by the injury such self-indulgence would inflict on an audience.

Artists: never stop believing that others believe in you.

Altruism in art is the most perfect form of vanity.

He compensated for his lack of accomplishments with extreme arrogance.

Artists should learn to tame the impulse to incessantly speak about themselves.

No artist has yet considered suicide as an artwork because to do so would require an abnormal absence of ego, not usually found in an artist.

Calling attention to oneself is easy; what is difficult is to merit that attention.

I knew a nobody who put himself at the center of every important photograph. For that remarkable ability, countless nobodies then sought to be photographed with him.

We love to nourish the myth that there are artists who require no explanation.

If we are making art only for ourselves, we should keep it to ourselves.

There is nothing more difficult to overcome than being told that you are great.

The best that can be said is that his interest in his own work is sincere.

Our greatest desire as artists has nothing to do with recognition, but with the thrill of knowing something others don't.

He was so much in love with his technical prowess that it became the subject of his work.

It is not self-consciousness that is perceived as a sin but the lack of it.

It is important to appear unaware of our best qualities so that others will discover them and tell the world all about us.

The quality of our flaws is as important as the quality of our talent.

In the same way one appears fatter in photographs, we appear to be worse artists when colleagues talk about our work.

The greatest barrier to the public's understanding of an artist is how much the artist struggles to be a member of the public.

Beware of revealing your self— but more importantly, beware of revealing your self-doubts.

VIII

Inspiration can't be imposed by law.

Creative tensions are not meant to be resolved.

Everyone is capable of creativity just like everyone is capable of loving. But it does not follow that everyone is capable of loving the result of everyone's creativity.

The more imprisoned you are by life, the greater the incentive to create.

Experiencing the process of drawing, painting or printmaking is pleasurable at first, but when we become experts it is all about agony.

The Blue Moon principle: everything we do as artists needs to appear to be a portentous anomaly and break with everything that came before.

"There are two sides to every question", but artists find new sides to every question.

It is a pity there are irreconcilable differences between being a great connoisseur and being original.

The worst moments of the creative process are those that others romanticize.

We lock ourselves in a garden imagining it to be a forest.

The most original actions come from commonplace ideas, but some of the most original ideas result in commonplace actions.

We all have, and should, protect the right to not make anything creative, but to praise lack of creativity is hypocritical.

What is the equivalent of a phantom limb in art?

We create imaginary worlds so that we can destroy them with impunity.

We should go "back to our roots" only to create something with different roots.

There is no such thing as appropriation. The minute we place an object or image into another context, it becomes transformed. But this means nothing if we do not notice.

The most important statement is what cannot be put into words.

What would be the equivalent of learning a foreign language in art?

A key requisite for creativity is to engage in a pointless activity.

Moderation is only dangerous when used in excess.

The most dangerous approach is inaction.

The best ideas are those we thought in passing but have yet to act on.

The two rules of artistic research are, first, that we do not know what we are looking for, and second, that we always end up finding something else.

To refrain from exhibiting is harder than exhibiting.

Leaving nothing to the imagination is a successful strategy only in pornography.

As we grow and struggle to become artists, we realize the most important conditions are out of our control—talent and obsession.

He figured that since quality was missing, he could at least overwhelm the world with quantity.

He only had one idea in his life, yet managed to create a thousand variations of it.

Envy is easily confused with inspiration.

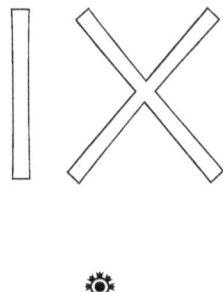

When it comes to socially-conscious art, the art world behaves like a country club doing charity work.

Dear Lord, thanks for all the blessings you have given me: a brutal professional environment where no one recognizes my efforts, where colleagues want me to fail, where predatory individuals want to take advantage of my good faith. Without all this my creativity and critical skills would have disappeared.

We fight throughout the night, encountering unimaginable beasts and dangers. The following morning there is a symposium chronicling what happened, questioning our every move.

Transgression was a necessity before it was a fashion.

When you are asked for an artist's statement, are they insinuating you are now an emerging artist?

When we see something stupid and hesitate to condemn it, it is because it might one day be regarded as visionary, and then we'd be remembered as stupid.

It is the charlatans that we should take seriously.

Before the 20th century, irony in art was the vocation of the few; since then we have spent a century overcompensating.

We make work that is consistent with our personal criteria and rigor, but are we ready to defend the consequences of this very criteria?

I met with a collection of formalists, conceptualists and political artists who believed in a nondenominational aesthetic. (It was just a dream.)

We have exchanged the individual genius for the genius of the mob.

Those who expect art to entertain deserve discomfort.

The best defense of the plagiarist is to retroactively claim irony.

We break the norms in order to be praised; we go away in order to be called back: art today benefits mainly from reverse psychology.

Beware of the artist's attempt to fully account for the intricacies of his or her artistic practice. The very need to do so is a sign that it is in trouble.

Every artist desires their own Boswell.

He was a classicist who knew that he would get nowhere being a classicist.

Whenever you believe the artwork is speaking to you, keep in mind, you are just speaking to yourself.

His was a great example of a "found art career."

Flattery is the sincerest form of performance art.

Generosity is old-fashioned.

She was relentlessly accusatory so she could hide her own faults.

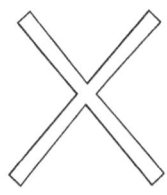

Not everyone is an artist, but everyone is a self-promoter.

The world will come to an end and I still haven't updated my CV.

Good art is all about management.

Branding the idea is more important than the idea itself.

Never sign, just give your word with a smile.

Eradicate consumers.

His art was about the impossibility of selling an art work.

Those who are ignorant may be the more knowledgeable ones.

There is a very fine line between collecting and hoarding.

It is easy to be an artist, i.e., delusional, narcissistic, self-centered.

What matters is the perception that work is actually being made.

To be spontaneous is not professional.

Like most successful companies today, the most important artwork is a system of distribution.

Never judge a work of art by its cover, but by who is collecting it.

A rose by any other name would smell as sweet, but it would probably have less value at auction.

The experienced arts professional is adept at speed dating.

He felt the need to fight the concept of "normal" every step of the way, except when he was talking to collectors.

It is the cult of the individual and the inability to understand Marx's notion of labor, that makes the art world think the free market is a natural law.

He failed in art history but succeeded in business.

The noise that an artist makes is the ambient sound of the art world.

Professional artists are suspicious of any pleasure they derive from making art.

The best ideas rise to the top regardless of who originated them.

For the corporate man, experiencing art is liberating. This reminds us of the time before art was corporatized.

The ideal of branding is when the artist stops producing good work and the market doesn't notice.

Art making may be an expression of liberty, but there is nothing like the imposition of a deadline to get things done.

Those who purchase names to amass an art collection should instead purchase hedge funds.

The expectation that we open a new exhibition and unveil a new project every week makes everything we have done ancient history.

It is only the successful artist who finds dignity in leaving the art world.

How can we think we understand the outside if our descriptions come only from the inside?

It's probably not an answer but a pitch.

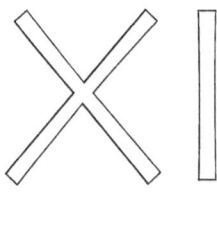

Conceptualism has become the folk art of the educated.

The 1960s is our new classicism.

If narratives disappear, so will the tyranny of time.

The most important questions today could never have been asked in the past.

Because anything can be art, we have to impose a value system.

The downside of being part of the conversation is it chains us to those conversations.

There once was a man who aimed to become the best art viewer in the world. He took every art history class and read every book of theory. As he learned to discriminate and expound on what was good vs. bad, gaining an impeccable eye and enviable taste, he grew depressed, lost all interest in art, and stopped going out. One day he was hit by a bus and lost all memory of his art education. No longer depressed, from that point on he was seen at every gallery, museum, and exhibition and celebrated as: "The happiest man in the art world".

The entirety of art history, when treated as a morality tale, is only as valuable as an elevator pitch.

While it is easy to see the wounds of the past, we often miss what is most wounding about the present.

We are always the hand maiden of a deceased artist.

Being alive is an advantage.

You are breaking new ground when there is no name for what you are doing. The moment it is named, it is time to do something else.

Contemporary art is another name for Stockholm Syndrome.

Turn your frustrations into humor, your sadness into irony, your anger into high-mindedness, and you will become a great artist of the 21st century.

Everyday we declare yet another thing is not art, is a loss to art history.

What counts is to invent the next language, not master the old.

Art is a gentrified neighborhood where everyone covets the last remaining dark alley.

Camus once said that the task of his generation was to prevent the world from destroying itself. Our generation's task is to build upon the ruins of their destructions.

Picasso was the singular genius of his generation because the art world was much smaller then.

There is nothing revolutionary about relying on the ideas of old revolutions.

An artist proposes, art history disposes.

Artists make a mess; art historians clean up after them.

Those who can't make art history falsify it.

Turn your influences into advantages.

He rebelled against everything, with the exception of the rising prices of his works.

Hypocrisy disguised as politeness is the best policy.

In conceptual art it there is no such thing as "easier said than done" because in conceptual art saying is doing.

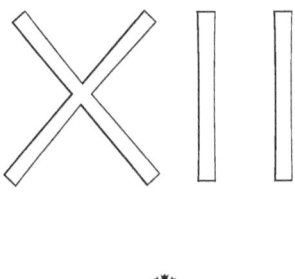

"I also used to do performance art when I was young", said the performance artist, as if it had been a phase that they overcame, when in reality, they never overcame the pull of their conservative values.

Stages of progression: when young the artist takes things literally, by middle age he sees everything with irony and detachment, until post mid-career, when he finally understands being literal is the best form of detachment.

Tolerance for the interminable is the true test of maturity.

We don't need to learn to draw like a child. We need to imagine like a child.

Be everyone you can possibly be until you get tired.

His greatest enemy was his younger self.

Challenging art, when realized poorly, is never as irritating as banal ideas realized with high production values.

Images are the progenitors of words, but once the words appear, images become the older relative—handicapped and in need of care.

He was young but projected the gravitas of an old man. In other words, he was an expert at condescension.

Young artists want to do things for the world. Older artists want the world to do things for them.

Being asked for an artist's statement when one has reached a certain age generates a similar puzzlement to getting carded in a bar.

When young he was an *enfant terrible*; by fifty he was an *artiste terrible*.

Artists fight their whole lives to become the artists that younger artists will fight their whole lives to replace.

Praise for a dying movement published in *The New York Times* is like the praise of an old Brooklyn restaurant that will soon be closed for good.

It is simpler for the aging artist to see the atrophying of their body then of their ideas.

When we hear someone say "My four year old could have made this" ask, "But could your four year old have come up with the problem?"

The task of the next generation of artists will be to solve the conflict between high-mindedness and critical rebellion.

They were condemned to become the children of a famous artist.

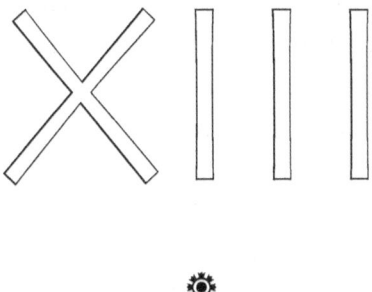

That which is not spoken is political.

Artists are just like politicians: the most successful get their message out soonest.

The concerns may be aesthetic but the argument is political. It rarely ever operates the other way around.

Chomsky reminds us, if people can be so knowledgeable about sports and have an opinion without being experts, the same should be applicable to political debate. Why not say the same thing about art? Because debates in art are not entertainment, and neither does art have the real-life effect that politics have.

Power is predicated on a very fragile collective opinion.

We want others to be radical as long as their actions don't interfere with our everyday lives.

Nothing is more inspiring to art than authoritarianism.

We should feel rewarded by our lack of satisfaction.

Artworks are more meaningful as illegal immigrants than as fully documented citizens.

Manifestos are no longer in vogue because we cannot unite behind an artistic idea we would die for.

Art used to be concerned with life and death; now it is only concerned with lifestyle.

Nationality is not content.

We can become better artists once we know the weaknesses of others.

If we want to influence those in power, we need to hit them where they are loneliest.

The art world encourages progressive ideas with conservative means.

We can put forth the most preposterous idea for an artwork, yet not even consider a minor reorganization of the social system of art.

Artists are encouraged to do unorthodox things as long as their means to this end are orthodox.

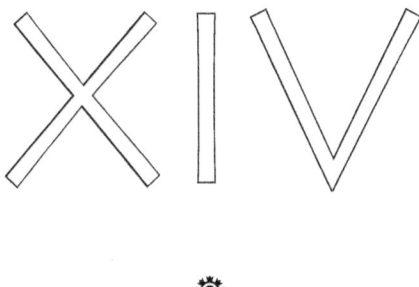

Ideas in the art discourse are generally very simple; what makes them complicated is our elaborate rituals of hiding their simplicity.

We should abandon any hope for mercy when judgments are objective, but we need to abandon any hope for quality when judgments are subjective.

If every opinion is valid, then the opinion that not all opinions are valid is valid.

The truth may be so hurtful that it may then be considered unimportant.

The concept of nothing can never be represented. The pretentious claims of doing so is usually what we see in its stead.

There is no conclusion or opinion about art without someone replying, "It depends on the circumstances" or "It depends on the artist". Could we ever arrive at a moment where variables are irrelevant? I guess it depends.

Messy thinking can produce clarity.

It is easier to lie with truth than with fiction.

Everything depends on the meaning of: "everything", "depends", "meaning", "on", "the" and "of".

We need everyone to know *what* it is, some know *how* it is, but no one *has* to know *why* it is.

They criticize Borges for popularizing and simplifying Swedenborg—as if Swedenborg is readable today.

The most difficult thing to achieve is not overcoming the opinions and influences of others, but finding meaning in our own creative loneliness.

Popularizes of art threaten art world insiders because they expose the very codes of taste they use to elevate themselves over others.

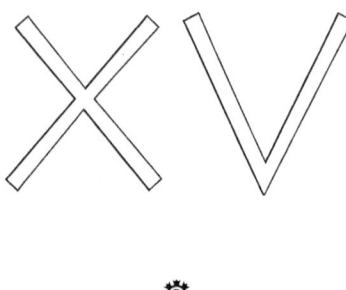

The path toward oblivion starts with people not answering your emails.

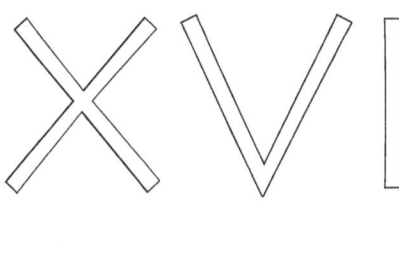

That which we never speak about is the most urgent thing to discuss.

If someone "disagrees" with an artwork it is because we have failed to disguise our politics.

He was so sophisticated that in the end he was unable to create.

Beware the artist who uses teaching as revenge.

An artist with a PhD becomes suspicious not because of the academic validity of the degree, but because of the implication that artistic excellence can be measured and codified academically.

The press takes itself very seriously—so seriously that it doesn't consider art seriously enough.

He was exposed to so much art that he became immune to it.

Our greatest misfortunes come from not understanding the conflation between words and actions.

If there are no right or wrong answers, why should there be right or wrong questions?

Understanding art is underrated.

An artwork needs to be thought to exist.

We need a manifesto of somnambulist art.

There used to be a time when art oscillated between academia and individuality. Today we have a system of art that oscillates between empiricism and ethnography.

Truth in art is ugly.

Matisse: Artists need to cut their tongues.
The present: Artists speak in many tongues.

Words are mightier than installation art.

We spend years learning the codes of visual art only to learn what is really needed are different codes.

Excess knowledge impedes action.

The debate around what is good art conflicts with the universal consensus of what is bad art.

Sor Juana, unable to access the nascent knowledge of the modern era, studied Hermetism. Today we often appear to be equally isolated and unable to discover the ideas of the present, not because we are unable to reach them, like Sor Juana, but because we are drowning in a sea of information.

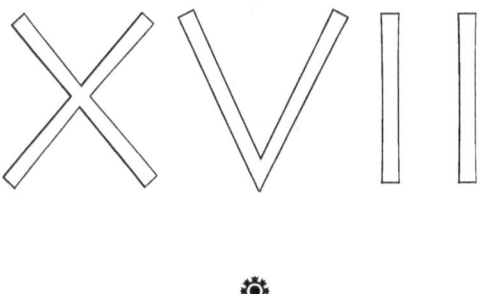

When pushing your own agenda, it is of utmost importance to present yourself as open-minded and inclusive.

Who invented the idea that what is good for a handful of people must be good for the masses?

*

The benefits of art should touch many, even if it is not meant to touch them.

Elitism for the masses!

If an artist only produces for himself or herself, they are still producing for a multitude.

The fact that an artwork can't make everyone happy is an advantage.

Wilde: "Be yourself—the others are taken" would be a sound phrase, only that the others are what constitute our self.

We can only claim authenticity through dishonesty.

An artist's work should feel like home—with all the positive and negative aspects this may entail.

We are living in the age of the death of the author because we have all become one.

All we need to do to produce bad artists is to give them lots of freedom and not enough things to be angry about.

XVIII

A world dominated by happiness is not possible; what is possible is a world where we can coexist successfully with sadness.

Nothing could be more oppressive than the demand to laugh.

One has to be simultaneously brutal and subtle.

Our happiness lies entirely in finding intentionality in everything.

It is always much riskier to show enthusiasm than skepticism.

The ability to be profoundly moved by art is the one advantage that amateurs have over experts.

Artists can be defined as individuals who never stop believing in fairy tales.

The appreciation of art lies exclusively with who owns the realization that something indeed is joyful.

We would so love it if our lives were an epic movie, yet there is nothing more deadly than living our life as if it were that epic movie.

Beware of those who share their emotions too readily.

Sincerity is something we only appreciate in household pets.

I make art because there is something I have lost and have no idea how to recover it.

It comes when we least expect it, not when we look for it.

The perfection of his life took away all his artistic ideas.

Pascal said that the source of our unhappiness is not knowing how to stay quiet in our room. It could be said that the source of an artist's unhappiness is not knowing how to stay quiet in the studio.

It is better to experience the frustration of engaging with the world than to withdraw and become the victim of your own reason.

The closest version of happiness is permanent dissatisfaction.

Art that relies heavily on democratic arguments to justify its existence is serving selfish purposes.

Great artworks are born from flaws.

We suffer when we miscalculate the consequences of defeat but not because we are surprised by defeat.

Eccentrics don't need the art world.

He made negativity into a style.

The Belgian historian Henri Pirenne was jailed by the Germans during World War I, where he wrote his masterwork—*History of Europe*—published after his death. I doubt any of us would like to go to prison to support our creative endeavors but the limitations or denial of privileges are more consequential to creativity than the abundance of perks of a comfortable life.

The need for art in a time of tragedy turns the artist into an ambulance chaser.

People love thinking of artists as crazy because they can't conceive that their understanding of normalcy is actually what is crazy.

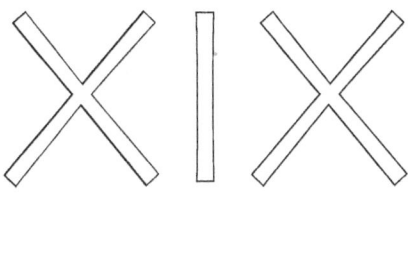

Shouldn't we have a publication that reviews and evaluates art critics?

If a curator has never experienced the process of making an artwork, what qualifies this person to speak so authoritatively about "process"?

*

The curatorial profession is no different than a librarian's.

It is too bad that most critics are critics of art as product, not as process.

If artists want to define themselves in their own terms they need to master the verbal dimension of their practice.

Be grateful of the notoriety that devastating critiques give you.

There should be a Viewer Museum that studies visitors to assess how successfully they understand and relate to what they see: Did they do a good job looking at the exhibition? Did they pay attention?

A completely unpredictable artist is too risky for a curator.

The Anti-Intentionalist Biennial: An exhibition of objects, environments, and circumstances debated as art works.

It is easy to call for the dismantling of the system. What is difficult is to make the system work.

The donkey played the flute.

I have never opened a quantum physics book in the middle of it and declared "this is not physics".

He remained anti-establishment even after he became the establishment himself.

I have always depended on the unkind criticism of strangers.

I wish artists knew, when talking to institutions, they are talking to the void.

We don't need institutions to think for us because they are not meant to think.

Everyone is entitled to their ignorance.

One of the least known aspects of the Apocalypse is that it will include the presentation of an interminable symposium with thousands of scholarly lectures.

The curator is closer to a Comp. Lit. scholar than an artist.

All normal standards of judgment cease to operate with those who are in love with art criticism.

Artists believe they are the center of the universe. Critics and curators think they are the creators of the universe.

Art institutions should do a better job of forbidding the art they hope can become more desirable.

The experienced artist finds critique in every compliment, and compliments in every critique.

If you have nothing to say you tell others what to do.

We learn more from our detractors than from our supporters.

We are conditioned to use criticism to give preference to the ends, not the means.

Art criticism is never as lame as when it is called art.

He took criticism of his work very seriously—more seriously than the work itself.

Never disregard a critic just because their review of your work is positive.

How often is the review worse than the artwork?

The occasion for the exhibition was merely the preview.

The hostile critic is the best partner one can have in art; at least we know their attitude is not hypocritical.

He set out to create a museum of artists' biographies.

He worked with a dead artist because he didn't want to be told how to curate, only to end up subjected to the advice of two dozen living art historians.

Exhibition catalogue essays are like the exhibitions they address: glanced at but not read.

Aim to be critically uplifting.

Give me as much clarity of purpose and politics as possible, so that I may critique and dismiss it.

What if a large art museum made a full exhibition about a non-artist?

Creating from scratch is agonizing; criticizing what exists is endlessly fun.

One has to admire those lecturers who captivate their audience with form while providing no content.

A connoisseur uses vast knowledge of a subject to police the things that enter it.

Art works function less as opinions than as generators of opinions.

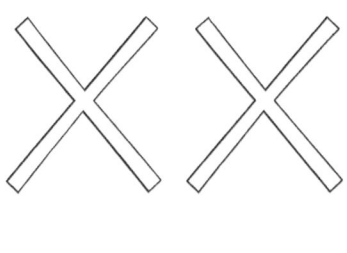

Someone once told me that the best way to collaborate is to impose one's will on others.

The easiest path for an artist is to be difficult.

The key lies in never doing the things you say you do.

The more demanding we are, the stronger is our position, as long as we can endure the demands of our demanding.

He made a brilliant career out of destroying the works of others.

Show me a great artist and I will show you a collection of ruined lives.

We may one day become more important than those who currently address us with condescension.

When experiences created by artists are described as "holistic" this means that they will fail to deliver any concrete expectations.

We should always welcome impertinence in art.

His artistic practice was predicated on making life impossible for others.

His refusal to say hello is his way of flirting.

Hatred is difficult to sublimate with nuance.

XXI

❂

Righteousness puts us in a strong place morally, but in a weak place artistically.

❂

One day there may be an artwork that does not need to be conceived to exist.

❂

Art is the only religion with rotating gods.

❂

True martyrdom consists in never allowing ourselves to take any chances.

Art can only change the world by being more than art.

The distrust of art is the one thing that can provide us with peace of mind.

We define ourselves not by what we reject, but by what we embrace.

Even if wrong, the artist with convictions is better than the artist who lacks any.

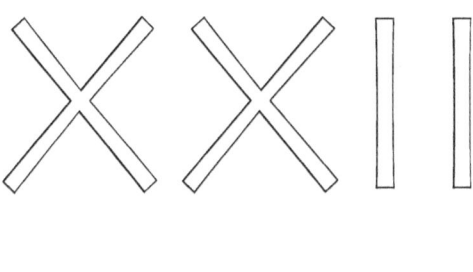

Since he wasn't able to resolve a project artistically, he opted for theorizing it.

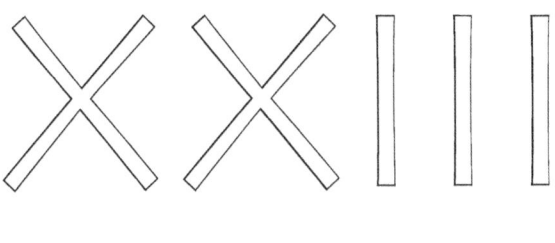

When put in the position of servicing anyone in the art world, we are subjected to conditions of coercion.

We know that we have made something significant when it enters the imagination of others.

The powerless want to attract attention, while the powerful want to stay hidden.

We never acknowledge the gifts we receive from censors, repressive governments and those who actively prevent art from happening. They are more important than those who actively give money and support.

As our attention spans shrink, we must make art more demanding.

Art should be equal parts masochism and hedonism.

We don't need to talk about good or bad art anymore, but of consequential and inconsequential acts of creativity.

We don't mature by becoming better communicators but by becoming better at restraining ourselves.

We should redouble our efforts to produce a shortage of artists.

One can help us best by never giving us what we want.

Our true challenge is to be absent with the strongest presence.

Invent a philosophy of art that applies to the one work you have made.

Art is profitable to the degree that it enhances the self-esteem of those with endless resources to buy it.

There are kinds of art that force their way into our lives whether we want them to or not, like the person at the party who keeps repeating himself over and over again at at the top of his lungs.

His work never made money, but many made money by writing about it.

Yell and repeat until it sounds rational.

The key to collaboration is making your collaborators think they came up with all the ideas.

That Mexico City tendency from a certain generation: exerting pressure on you to agree by looking at you with the gravest expression possible.

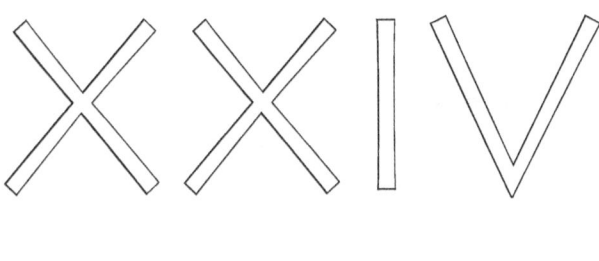

On the day he was showered with praise, he was sincere and replied: "I agree, with you, I am exceptional." After that, the praise diminished.

His gratitude revealed how small he felt.

We need someone whose foibles make him or her a credible figure.

We can't pretend to be immune to what the world thinks of us.

When we get praise, it is never enough.

Nobody likes someone more than those who have thrown themselves into lost causes.

We must eat to live, not live to eat. We must make art to live, not to make a living.

An artist can never be indifferent to the works of others.

For an artist, making art is never on the list of priorities; it is a given.

Her stick figures were so poorly drawn that her friends celebrated her conceptual rigor.

XXV

We expect artists to make good, but we don't expect them to be good.

Playing the devil's advocate means never having to take a position.

He aspired to being more unethical than he ever turned out to be.

Apply enough ethical standards to the making of art and we will abolish it altogether.

It is not bad because it is unethical, but its lack of ethics gets in the way of finding other means to interpret it.

Be careful when you meet artists; you may end up becoming material for their work.

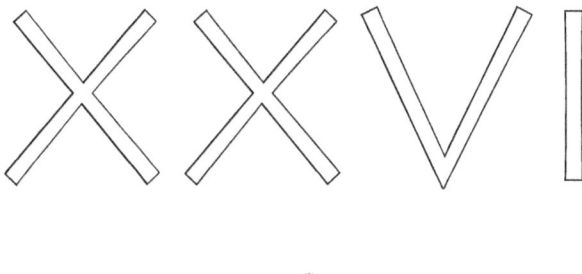

Saying the right thing in front of an artwork can save its life.

It should surprise nobody that at some point we can't recognize the difference between the living and the dead.

❂

Our most important chapters in life contain a degree of disassociation.

Apparently in certain historical periods artists were more prone to commit suicide. Were they living at a time when art mattered more?

Performance artworks should be treated like people.

In order to make great work he felt he needed more drama in his life. He moved to a war-torn country, let his personal life fall apart, and was dead within two years. It never occurred to him that the art he was making would never be considered great art.

XXVII

He traveled so much he stopped noticing differences between places. It was not that the places were the same but that he had become desensitized to change.

Artists are card-carrying citizens of the Republic of Contemporary Art.

Duchamp and Picasso are lucky to have never been subjected to today's social media and the 24 hour news cycle.

We dismiss the capitals of the art world under the belief that relevant art can be made anywhere in the world. But that which is relevant art in an art capital may be irrelevant in a small town and vice versa.

We think we would be happier in a smaller world with less competition until we realize it is in small communities that competition is born.

Do not despair: bigotry still exists everywhere we look.

XXVIII

Hippocrates wrote: "Life is short, art long, opportunity fleeting, experience deceptive, judgment difficult." Today art is fleeting, opportunity difficult, and judgment easy.

Swift: "A sign of a true genius is that all the dunces are in confederacy against him." It should be noted, often a confederacy of dunces is what goes against another dunce.

John Barrymore once said: "My only regret is that I was never able to descend from the stage to watch myself perform." Shouldn't that be a relief?

Francis Bacon observed: "Solomon saith: *There are no new things upon the earth*. So that as Plato had an imagination, *that all knowledge was but remembrance*; so Solomon giveth his sentence, that all novelty is but oblivion." And so, the act of making art is an act of misremembering so that others can remember.

Canetti: "Explain nothing. Put it there. Say it. Leave." He forgot to add: "Peek in from your hiding spot to see if everyone is talking about it."

Henry de Montherlant: "Stupidity consists not in not having ideas but in having lots of stupid ideas." Similarly, bad artists are not those who don't know what to make, but who make too much of what it is they know how to make.

Epictetus: "Never say about anything that it has been lost, but that it has been restored." In other words, when you are rejected from an exhibition, or denied an award, say, "Now my lack of importance has been restored."

The greatest art is measured not in what it shows but in what it conceals. So we should strive to be the first ones to conceal what it is people are waiting to hear.

Thomas Jefferson: "In matters of principle stand like a rock; in matters of taste swim with the current." Had he been an artist, he would have realized that in art, matters of taste *are* matters of principle.

"The best ideas are common property" says Seneca. So are the worst ideas.

Cowper: "God made the country, and man made the town." Duchamp made Conceptual Art, and later artists made their own provincial versions.

Thoreau: "We are sculptors and painters, and our material is our own flesh and bones." We are also short order cooks whose oeuvre is greasy French fries.

Glossary

Agree
The behavior of acquaintances at an opening before they separate and criticize one another.

Age
What artists complain about but exploit at every stage they are at.

Ageless
How collectors behave.

Alacrity
When one mentions the bad review of a rival and is compassionate.

Ancient
Yesterdays' vernissage.

Ambition
When one is more interested in what's next rather than what's already occurred.

Art Fair
The land of lost content.

Artless
A social practice project.

Awareness
To be conscious, but not overly.

Awful
Works defended by saying "taste is subjective".

Biography
The personal history of those who never made mistakes.

Blameless
Postmodernists.

Bitter
The feeling one gets when looking at a work that looks exactly like what you just made.

Bubble
When the studio becomes one's mirror of the world.

Calm
Frantically looking for attention and recognition, as if these things were oxygen.

Career
The temptation to submit to what is in fashion.

Clairvoyance
Art that is nothing more than a statement about the present, later on found to be true.

Commitment
As they say about arranged marriages "Love comes later."

Compensate
When we maximize the minimal.

Contract
Art appreciation for lawyers.

Council
Great wisdom that no longer applies to younger artists.

Debase
To minimize the work that completely defines our thinking and aesthetics.

Debt
The pain other artists went through so we can complain about all they left out.

Empathy
What others feel who have made equally terrible works.

Everlasting
Resentment.

Experience
What we don't recognize until we are stuck in the middle of it.

Eye
Old-fashioned tool once used to look at art, currently used to read exhibition labels.

Feeling
The state of senselessness one experiences from trying to make a good artwork.

Fleeting
A good review.

Fuel
What visitors are for the art museum.

Generosity
The act of giving worthless gifts to others.

Influence
He was a sacred cow in his town. Outside of it, he was only a cow.

Interpretation
The process of providing facts, stories and theories about an artwork that are forgotten a few hours later.

Introspection
What those who are established in the art world eventually forget to use.

Leadership
Critics as self-designated drivers who have never learned to drive.

Lustruous
The artist who is discovered today and forgotten tomorrow.

Mail
Physical exhibition invitations—used to primarily be a means of communication; now they primarily are a sign of status.

Match
Artist couples who hate the same curator.

Measured
The artist who does an overview of his entire career when invited to speak for five minutes.

Multitude
What the dealer who has not sold a single work is referring to when he says, "There is a lot of interest."

Narrative
What everyone is trying to snatch away from an another.

Nearsightedness
Action of traveling all over the world to biennials and art fairs in exotic locations, buying the work of the same five artists who live next door.

Nonsense
Ideas that are deemed good because they are complicated.

Occupation
What you need in order to be an artist.

Opinion
Hating all art.

Packaging
What everyone learns in art school.

Persuasion
The intensity of your conviction regardless of whether it is true.

Prank
An artistic medium taught in the academy along with egg tempera.

Professional
Someone whose specialty is questioning everyone else's art.

Querulous
What someone is who knows nothing about art.

Radical
Artists who paint still lives in the style of old masters.

Reciprocity
To admire and be admired by those we do not respect.

Reading
What seeing used to be.

Rent
What requires artists to accept unsavory professional commitments.

Repetition
A powerful approach, until it is repeated by everyone.

Research
Ingredient used to appear scholarly.

Restrained
A collecting frenzy.

Ruinous
To change your style.

Sanguine
The dealer with no sales in the last hour of the art fair.

Seminal
A indelible academic remnant of pre-feminist art history.

About the Author

In a methodical way and recurring to strategies connected to the baroque fugue and ars combinatoria (combinatory art), Pablo Helguera (Mexico City, 1971) often draws improbable relationships between human histories, biographies, anecdotes and historical events, always bringing them all together in a cohesive whole and making all serve as a reflection on our current relationship with art as a society. Helguera often focuses on history, pedagogy, sociolinguistics and anthropology in formats such as lectures, museum displays, performance and written fiction. His project *The School of Panamerican Unrest* (2003–2011), an early example of pedagogically-focused socially engaged art, consisted in a nomadic think-tank, physically crossed the continent by car from Anchorage to Tierra del Fuego. He has exhibited widely internationally (MoMA, Havana Biennial, Performa, Reina Sofia, amongst many others) and has been recipient of the Guggenheim, Franklin Furnace and Blade of Grass Fellowships and the Creative Capital and Art Matters grants. He was the first recipient of the International Award of Participatory Art of the Emilia Romagna Region in Italy. His book *Education for Socially Engaged Art* (2011), a primer for social practice has quickly become adopted as a main textbook for art schools and university programs internationally. He is also author of several other books including *The Pablo Helguera Manual of Contemporary Art Style, Theatrum Anatomicum (and other performance lectures)*,

What in the World, and *Art Scenes: The Social Scripts of the Art World*, a book on the sociology of contemporary art. In 2013 he launched the project *Librería Donceles*, consisting in creating the only Spanish used bookstore in New York, a non-profit project intended to draw attention to the perceptions of Latin American culture in the U.S.

He is married to artist Dannielle Tegeder and lives in Brooklyn.

Other books by Pablo Helguera

Endingness: Prolegomena for a New Art of Memory
The Pablo Helguera Manual of Contemporary Art Style
The Boy Inside the Letter
The Witches of Tepoztlán (*and Other Unpublished Operas*)
Artoons (*I, II, and III*)
The Juvenal Players
Suite Panamericana
Hacia una Estética de la Burocracia
Estela y las Hojas
Theatrum Anatomicum (*and Other Performance Lectures*)
The Juvenal Players
What in the World (*a Subjective Museum Biography*)
The School of Panamerican Unrest (*an Anthology of Documents*)—with Sara Demeuse
Urÿonstelaii
Education for Socially Engaged Art
Pedagogia No Campo Expandido—with Monica Hoff
Art Scenes: The Social Scripts of the Art World
Onda Corta
He Was Elan
Artunes
The Parable Conference

www.ingramcontent.com/pod-product-compliance
Lightning Source LLC
Chambersburg PA
CBHW020427220526
45464CB00002B/598